Jane Cadwallader

PB3
Recycles

Illustrated by Gustavo Mazali

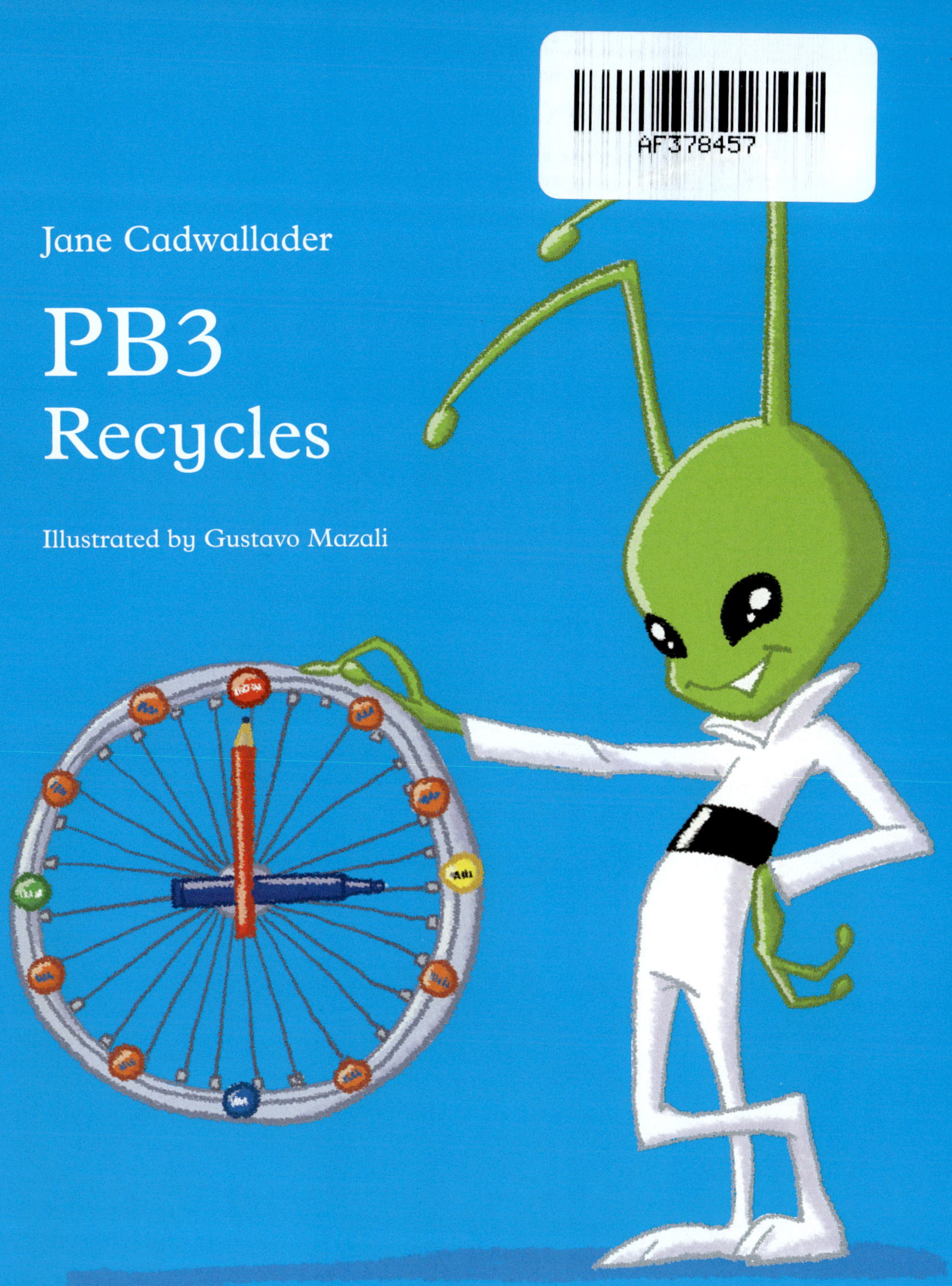

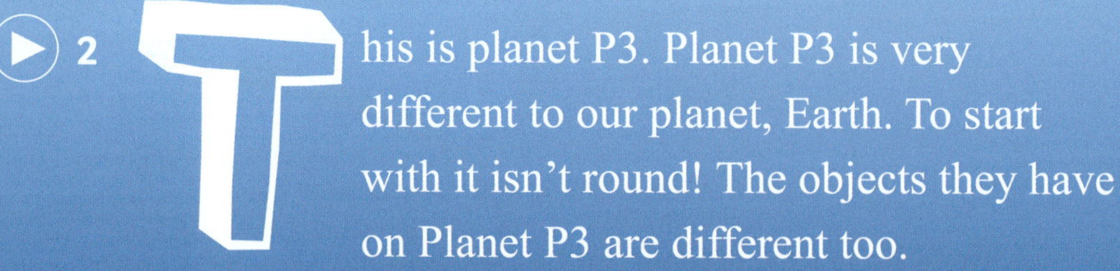

This is planet P3. Planet P3 is very different to our planet, Earth. To start with it isn't round! The objects they have on Planet P3 are different too.

They don't have apples or rivers or monkeys or clocks and … the only colours they have are grey, black, green and white.

Here is an E.T. from Planet P3. His name is PB3 and here is his robot, Robin … Oh dear! What's the matter with Robin? She's going round and round!

PB3 calls the doctor. The doctor gives Robin an injection and she stops going round and round.

PB3 and the doctor look inside Robin. The doctor takes out a needle. The needle is made of wood and not of metal. This is because Robin is an old robot. Now there are no trees on P3 and … the needle is broken. The doctor tells PB3 to throw Robin in the rubbish and buy a new robot.

NO! Robin is my friend! Where can I find trees?
Hmmm! The only planet with trees is Planet Earth.

PB3 puts Robin into his spaceship and he goes to
Planet Earth. He doesn't want to throw Robin in
the rubbish! He wants to find a needle made of
wood and he wants to help Robin!

PB3 goes to Mumbai in India. He taps on a window. Inside the room is a girl called Adi. Adi is very surprised to see an E.T. at the window!
tap!
tap! tap!

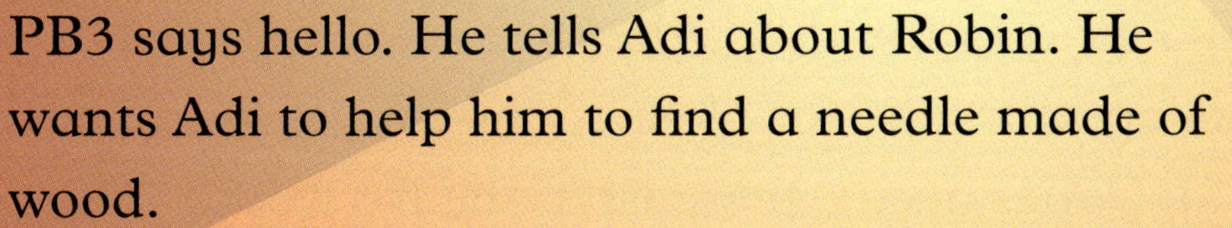

PB3 says hello. He tells Adi about Robin. He wants Adi to help him to find a needle made of wood.

On the road to the shops they see some coloured recycling bins: one for plastic, one for glass and one for paper but … there isn't one for wood!

They also see some children on a rubbish tip. They don't go to school. They collect things to sell. PB3 wants to talk to the children. But Adi doesn't want to talk to them.

Adi and PB3 go to a toy shop. It has dolls and balls and cars and games and monsters and planes. They go to a clothes shop. It has sweaters and shirts and trousers and coats. And they go to a supermarket. The supermarket has fruit and fish and meat and chairs and mirrors and cupboards and desks. In the shops Adi shows the broken needle.

I'm sorry.
We don't have
a needle made
of wood.
I'm sorry. We don't have
a needle made of wood.

Adi is sad. She doesn't know what to do!
I've got an idea!

They talk to the children collecting things to sell
on the rubbish tip. PB3 tells the children about
Robin. Adi isn't happy!

The children look and look and look. They are happy to help! PB3 looks too and … slowly Adi begins to look too! ■

▶ 3　*POEM*

We're looking here
We're looking there
We're looking really
Everywhere.

We're looking for a needle
That is made of wood
Anyone who finds it
Just shout GOOD! ■

4 Suddenly a small boy shouts. He is holding an old fishing net and …

PB3 puts the needle made of wood into Robin's
back and slowly Robin begins to move again!
She moves her neck, she moves her head, she
moves her arms. She moves her body.
Robin smiles! PB3 smiles too!

Robin wants to thank the children. She makes some coloured slime for them to play with. They are happy! Adi is talking to the older children.

It's time for PB3 and Robin to go home. They take photos of the recycling bins. They are going to start recycling on Planet P3! They are taking some trees too! Below on Earth the children are busy. What are they doing?

Oh look! Adi and the children have got first prize in the Rubbish to Treasure Competiton!

26

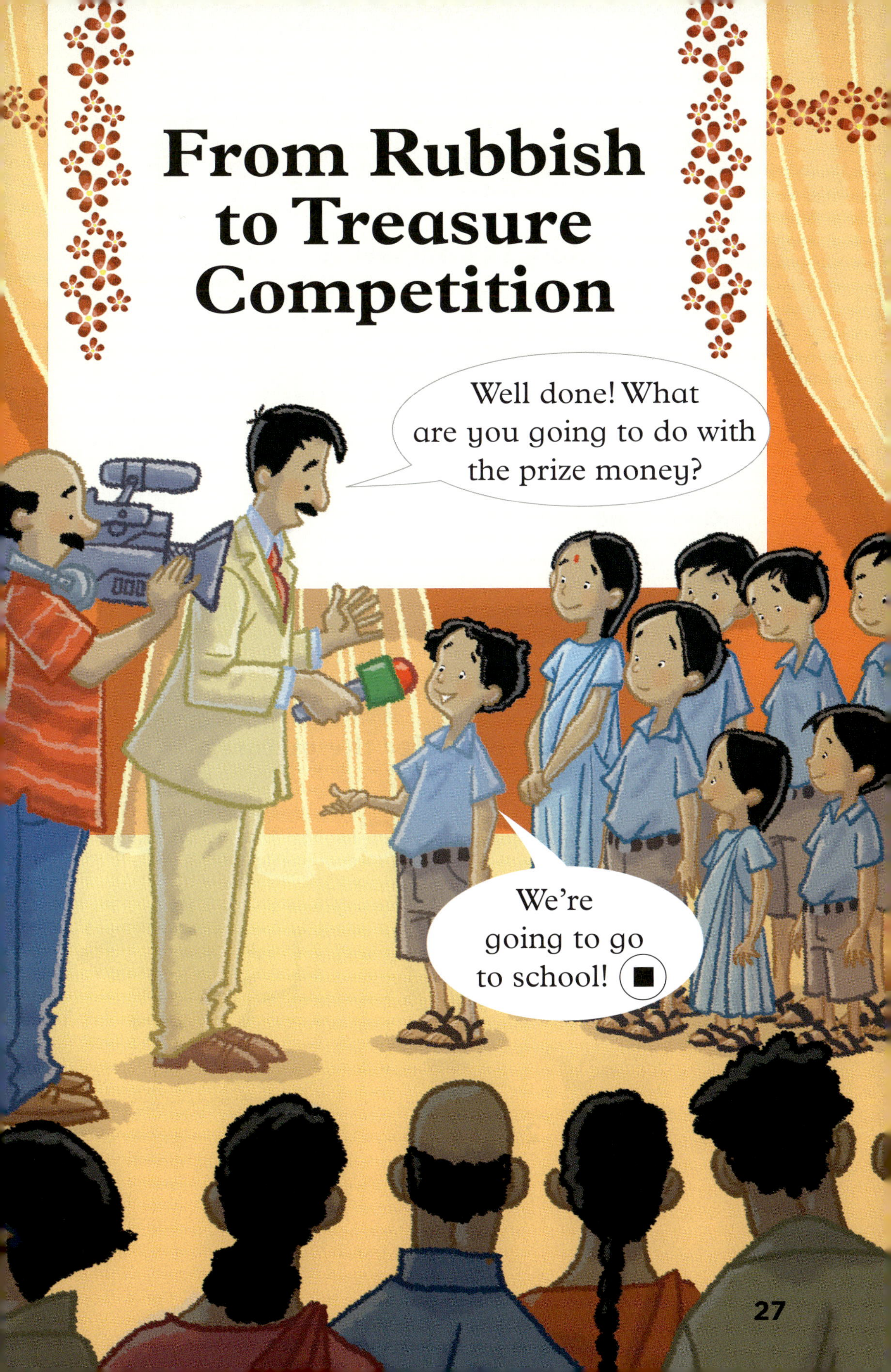

From Rubbish to Treasure Competition

1 **Match to find the names.**

1 ☐ An E.T. called		**a**	tip children
2 ☐ A robot called		**b**	assistants
3 ☐ An Indian girl called		**c**	journalist
4 ☐ The boy		**d**	from P3
5 ☐ The 3 shop		**e**	PB3
6 ☐ The television		**f**	Adi
7 ☐ The rubbish		**g**	Robin
8 ☐ The doctor		**h**	who finds the needle

2 **Write the names under the pictures.**

1

2

3

3 **Choose the words to finish the poem.**

We're looking ___________________
We're looking ___________________
We're looking really _____________ .

We're looking for a ______________
That is made of ________________ .
Anyone who finds it
Just shout ___________________ !

wood

needle

here

GOOD

there

everywhere

4 **Correct the mistakes.**

1 The doctor on P3 tells ~~Robin~~ ___PB3___ to throw ~~PB3~~ ___Robin___ in the rubbish.

2 PB3 goes to ~~P3~~ _________ to find a needle made of ~~plastic~~ _________ .

3 PB3 meets an Indian ~~boy~~ _________ called ~~Ali.~~ _________ .

4 Some children on a ~~planet~~ _________ help them.

5 The children are ~~sad~~ _________ to help.

6 PB3 puts the needle into Robin's ~~leg~~ _________ .

7 Robin makes some ~~orange~~ _________ slime.

8 The children get ~~second~~ _________ prize in the Rubbish to Treasure Competition.

9 They are going to use the money to go to ~~P3~~ _________ .

5 **Act out the following play with your friends.**

What you need:

- a needle and a broken needle made of wood
- a poster for the Competition
- a microphone for the journalist
- objects / drawings for the shops and rubbish tip
- drawing(s) of From Rubbish to Useful object(s)

(on Planet P3)
PB3: What's the matter with Robin?
Robin: I'm not fine! I'm not fine! I'm not fine!
P3 doctor: Look, this needle is broken.
It's made of wood and we don't have trees
now on P3. Throw the robot in the rubbish!
PB3: NO! NO! NO! Not my Robin! Where
can I find trees?
P3 doctor: On planet Earth.

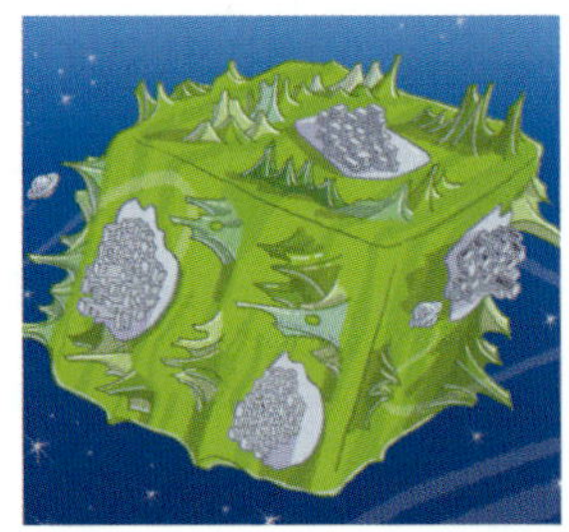

(journey to Earth)
(on Earth, at Adi's house)
Tap tap tap
PB3: Hello. I'm PB3.
Adi: OH! Hello. My name is Adi.
PB3: Can you help me? I want to find
a needle made of wood for my robot.
Adi: Hmmm. Let's go to the shops.

(in the shops)
Shop assistants 1, 2, 3: I'm sorry. We don't have a needle made of wood.

(at the rubbish tip)
PB3: Let's ask the children to help.
Adi: Hmmm! They are very dirty!
PB3: Can you help us?
Children: YES!
All: the poem (see page 29)
Boy: GOOD! GOOD! GOOD! A needle made of wood!

(at Adi's house)
Robin: Here's something for you to play with.
Children: Thank you Robin! We want to go to school!
Adi (with poster of Competition): I've got an idea!

(at the competition)
Adi: We've got first prize.
Children: Hurrah!
Journalist: What are you going to do with the money?
Children: We are going to go to school! Hurrah!

6 Draw something made from recycled objects or materials. Describe it.

My recycled object is made of _______________________

It is useful / beautiful because _______________________

7 Do you like the story? Draw your face.

- 😄 I love the story!
- 🙂 I like the story.
- 🙂 I quite like the story.
- 😐 I don't like the story.